The Alleluia Tree

New and Selected Poems

by Christine Swanberg

The Puddin'head Press
2012

Dedication

For the support of these poets,
whose inspiration will be missed:
John Dickson,
Richard Calisch,
and Susan Bright.

Table Of Contents

The
Alleluia
Tree

You sit in the chiropractor's office waiting
to have your spine straightened and strengthened.
You're here because so many forces
have conspired to bring about your misalignment:
your first fall from the big Schwinn,
the accident that sent you rolling in a cornfield,
a lifetime of improper lifting,
the extra weight garnered slowly
to make up for the large girth of losses
the middle-aged mind readily conjures
before it begins its great journey of forgetting.
Perhaps you have no luck
with established therapies
and wish to ward off intentional wounds,
your scars already knit from misappropriated
cruelties, snares, and scrapes collected
on this blue, imperfect planet.
Yet here you are,
hopeful in your glorious misalignment,
still eager for healing
heading forward,
reading a recipe you might just try for dinner.
Misaligned or not, you stay the course,
despite the urn of mistakes sitting on your mantel.
My dear Misaligned, Mislocated, Misconstrued,
Mismanaged, and Mischievous,
it's You. You're the one
for whom I write these poems.

Heartland

I live in a city in the Heartland
where my domestic life blooms
with its garden of prairie grass,
perennials that return like distant friends,
and hummingbirds dart and dive.
I live in a marriage eclipsing four decades,
and a litany of rescued cats with ironic names.
Aidan Quinn once lived in my house,
but no one around here much cares
though I find that fact enchanting.

My Heartland home pleases me
with its logical feng shui, skylights,
marble fireplace, hardwood,
mosaic tiles, and poignant attention to 1950's chic.
I celebrate my home.
Nowhere else in America could I afford
this house, which I require for my well being.
I live in the city I was born in
though it was not my intention to do so.
I have left it countless times
for many great adventures which I cherish.

My entire small family lives here.
We are Italian and know how to cook.
Every one of us is a Democrat.
My family is Catholic; I am not.
I require old English hymns, gospel,
and a God that loves me no matter what
I have done or failed to do.
Protesting is a freedom I frequent.

I am happy, but not perfectly happy,
in this Heartland city with its big river
running through it, its community gardens,
its crumbling streets and schools.
It's not ideal here, yet the winter's quiet
is broken only by songs
of the hardy birds we feed without fail.
Just now a downy woodpecker hangs
upside-down at the suet from the sunset maple.

From Coal To Music

For George Ella Lyon

I rose from coal and caged canaries
singing at sunrise, and before that the shimmering sea
of the Adriatic, and the House of Seven Brothers.
I belong to long sea journeys that led to coal mines.

Then Wisconsin lakes and snow
taller than prairie grass, from "Pin the Tail
on the Donkey" to "Hail, Holy Queen,"
"Blue Suede Shoes" to "Venus in Blue Jeans."

I danced to Ricky Nelson and traded dog tags,
blessed by benevolent piano teachers and pink leotards,
carhopping and real chocolate malts,
'57 Chevies and Freddy Johnson's English Leather.

I wore candy stripes and served the sick,
ran drill presses at factory night shifts, suffered
coal black college nights and the Purple Haze of Vietnam.
I went to Woodstock and became the music.

I returned home and married a hometown guy
to "It Only Takes a Moment."
Let no man put asunder. Vows weaved magic.
Nearly forty years. No one has put us under.

I taught a hundred teenagers a day in a school thick
as a prison. Some arrived with hot coals in their fists.
"Jump. Go ahead and jump" screamed. Some did.
Yes, I rose from coal and music

to sea and mountain, true love and good work,
"Moonlight Sonata" and "California Dreamin,"
from Heartland, the City of Big Shoulders,
from coasts, dirt and dust, Lemon Pledge and diamonds.

Now when I sing "I Come to the Garden Alone"
in a small church choir of aging but fervent voices,
I can't say I understand a lick of it for sure, yet
the secret tug of destiny keeps polishing that coal.

Backroads

You like to be alone.
You camp,
watch moths burn
in wonder.
I see your brown corduroys,
your boots, leatherlaced,
your knees up.
You are contemplating
something I do not see.
I am driving my fast car
on these backroads
and know we would be friends.
I like to be alone,
but I am still turned
too inward.
I have not become
the moth, the fire,
the dirt in my nails.
But slowly, slowly,
I am becoming
this thin road,
this fog,
these sparse Midwest trees,
the squirrel and the crow.

A shooting star pierces
a field of wheat.
There is a crater
in my hand.
I want to turn toward you.
In our open palms
stars locked,
and I cannot unlock them.
The best I can do
is the worst I can do.
Accelerate.
Turn up the radio.
Drive home again.

Tonight, on this late road
when the sky is past indigo
and the stars are just there,
I light a cigarette
and blast the radio.
Van Halen screams:
Jump. Go ahead and jump.
My foot arches
against the pedal.
One hand grips the wheel.
I race the yellow line
and think of you again:
having to get somewhere
but not knowing where:
something like going home:
something about being lost
in a galaxy
that might be lost
in a universe.
I like to think
I know where I am going.
How hard for you
unable to say
who you are
or even pretend.

Bridges

My first memory of them is the Lincoln Bridge
that glides over the Illinois river in LaSalle-Peru,

a stretch between the coal mines of Spring Valley

and the green leafy canopies of elms
of the rich Northern city, where my father

escaped to find a better life. Forgive me—

I have always been thankful for his choice
not to live amongst the tree-barren shanties

of coal towns, mean old men, and small minds.

I too have no wish to return.
The bridge and the wide expanse of water

remain the only beauty I carry from that bleak place.

Yet I still seek bridges away from my Northern city
where the elms were slaughtered, canopies collapsed,

each and every one. Bridges stretch like hope,

transitions to a place you must go to save yourself.
When you find you are in some sad space,

think about the bridges you have already tread.

In the Ticino small, stone Roman bridges arch
over blue pools of mountain waters that rush

each spring when snow gushes from peaks.

In summer languid bathers stretch on rocks
beneath such bridges, the air so fresh and clean

it frees the breath. The Bridge of Lions crests

over the Matanzas River in St. Augustine,
where dolphins dance near boats with black sails.

Invoke the bridges you have known

when you seem stuck on a confounding shore.
Recall them: small bridges on winding roads

where only one car can pass at a time, or

magnificent bridges like the ones you find
in great cities. Call upon the one that stands

foremost above your mind's winding rivers.

Ask that bridge for the answer you seek.
See how it carries you on its sleek, steel spine?

Know that no matter how tense and turbulent

the waters spin, you want to keep living in a world
where bridges keep their promises:

they take you to the place you need to go.

Moonbeam And Starlock

When the fortune teller scowled
at your broken life-line, you laughed
in that shanty where wood incandesced
like red wands. The old Appalachian, wrinkled,
bald and bristled, whispered *Be careful.*
To me: *I see you at a desk.*

That night a gust blew our tent over
a cliff in the Smokies. You were amused.
I was terrified. You stayed cool
as a willow while my hands quivered
like aspens. As black leaves swirled
and roared, we huddled in the old Pontiac

and wrote notes on *Kleenex*:
    You who have known the storm, what secret
    are you howling?
                    Moonbeam
    The secret is in the eye of the storm,
    and you are it.
                    Starlock
We never made it to Mardis Gras

but twenty years later, little monks
in orange grow like great pumpkins
in your spirit patch, not far
from my carrots, quilled pens
pointed inward.

One day you see that you have crossed
the long, thin bridge of decades,
walking to the beat of the steadfast
drummer who runs the show
to the orchard on the other side.
Now pick the ripened fruit.
Bite into what you have reaped,
savoring each crunch,
and the bittersweet nectar.
You will not be expelled.
Because you have been true,
the garden is returned to you.

Lament For The Silent Sister

Suppose computers jumped over the moon
And cell phones floated unencumbered
Around Venus, or that Call Waiting suffered
A heart attack, and the third television lost
Its will to live. Suppose then all the people returned
From their great Distraction to welcome Unsplintered Silence,
As though it were a Prodigal Daughter.
Would we say: Oh, how we have missed you.
Come. It is the Mother's pleasure to prepare
A feast for you. O Silent Sister, welcome home?

Whenever I hear Rhapsody in Blue—
its high notes fluttering like cabbage moths,
its twisted and turbulent augmentations—
I feel the kind, thin, succulent-veined hand
of Mrs. Christiansen, my piano teacher,
brushing my right wrist,
settling like an elfin moth.
She's affirming my meager meanderings
on the cherry wood piano that smells
of Lemon Pledge. She's with me all the way
through Now-I-Start-With-Lesson-One,
Making-Music-is-Such-Fun to Blue Nocturne.
She's snapping her sallow, freckled fingers
to that Dog Gone Boogie
(which I probably put out of its misery).
She's nodding, tight-lipped and wide-eyed
as my short but nimble fingers flayed out
The Flight of the Bumble Bee
(the bee slightly tipsy).
Her hand is drawn up to her neck
during Autumn Leaves
(which I probably pruned the life out of).
Any Rimsky-Korsakov or Tchaikovsky
sent her into glazed over Buddhahood.
Dear Mrs. Christiansen, who recognized
another hopeless romantic when she saw one,
who had the good sense to know
I'd never make it to virtuoso. Because of her
I have loved the piano ever since,
no matter how unmagnificent the solos to my cat might be.
In those years before our bodies blistered out of control—
hers with cancer that turned her skin to beeswax,
mine ajar with hormones and pheromones so potent
I lost my taste for music and went fortissimo for boys—
we enjoyed each other's company,
bedazzled, drawn toward a startling luminescence.

Night Shift

You cannot get the metal shavings out.
You really have to wash behind your ears.
Even after showering you taste factory,
acquire a strong desire to spit,
hope no one is watching.

A man with bad teeth might hustle you.
When you say you're not interested,
he says, "Who do you think you are?
Everyone can see the dirt in your nails."
One night you count the holes: 1104.

You become the machine,
letting one hand think while the other
holds a book to your knee. Try to read
in that dim fluorescence with one eye
as the other stalks the foreman

who doesn't exactly catch you but says
the next night, "You scrapped a bunch.
Holes on the wrong side." He's nice,
pats you, says, "Never mind. Everyone
does that sometimes." You feel guilty.

In the morning you welcome honest humidity
and real light though they wrangle your sleep.
Your dreams are muffled in gray and grime.
Even the birds sound metallic. One night
you dream of a mammoth woodpecker, steel

with riveted joints and holes for eyes.
You wake and realize you don't know
what you are making all night at drill press.
The foreman says, "War parts."
You take off your goggles and go home.

The Contessa And I

Ever since a woman enrolled
in my writing class
because she thought I was
the Barefoot Contessa,
I find myself writing poems
about food and wine.

The resemblance is delectable:
brown saucy bobbed hair,
mischievous nutmeg eyes,
hands nimble as fruit pickers',
a reassuring melon roundness,
our peachy husbands, both Jeffreys.

No kids but nests full of freedom
to travel wherever we want,
sip espresso all over the world,
know our herbs and spices from a to z,
throw a good dinner party,
revel in excellent wines and pairings.

If barefoot is a metaphor for down-to-earth,
accessible, the opposite of well-heeled,
then sign me on as the Barefoot Poetess.
Though that would be stealing and cheesy,
I can't think of a better word than barefoot.
Perhaps the Contessa could stir up tastier.

Rearview Mirror

What does it matter
that a man in a blue truck,
old, rusted, and dented,
pulls off the side of the road,
yanks his dog out of the car
where she sat next to him
like some loyal goodtime gal
who can never get enough
but always gets too much,
then gets dumped
for maybe having too much heart
or not knowing
she has this annoying habit
see, like laughing too loud?
So what does it matter
that the dog cowers in the ditch
and won't leave
and the man takes off his belt
and beats
a little
until the bitch slinks away
in the snow, already sniffing
for homescent, confused,
as the man swerves off
and doesn't look back?

Ten Minutes On Michigan Avenue

A full moon loops
around Buckingham Fountain.
Horns muffle, evaporate
into Lake Michigan, holding
cement monoliths so bold
I wonder how a woman
could love this city.
The brusque wind has killed geraniums
potted in the sidewalk café's white boxes.
Sipping cappuccino, hot froth of milk,
surprising January splash of sun: Why
does this city comfort me,
small woman with a past
a hundred miles away?

Here I am the golden phoenix
of my dreams, drinking elixir
from a bone-white cup,
watching another woman
wearing a blue beret,
her face large, lunar and pale,
ruby lipstick startling as the siren
that slides from my periphery.
Anything can happen here;
Matisse to murder.
Sandburg's thumbprint
or a lighthouse blinking
under moonlight in the fog.

The Alleluia Tree

The epic blizzard tore and tumbled
through bare maples, grumbling locusts,
tilting pines and toppling prairie grass.
Nothing this severe since the early 70's.

We woke to Siberian drifts pressing
sliding doors, a deck slightly swayback,
skylights packed with snow thick as cement,
the holes of feeders and bird houses

rimmed with ice. Winter regulars struggled
to get their seeds, their feathers
puffed and coated with snow. I sang
a song of lamentation for the birds,

watching them grow invisible and silent.
A sudden drop to twenty below.
I feared the birds had perished,
and prayed for cryogenic miracles.

For over a week not one woodpecker,
cardinal, chickadee, junco, sparrow,
nor jay joined forces against the wind.
One poor sparrow finally dared

and soon became the breakfast of a silver hawk,
perched upon the fence like a winged gargoyle.
I prayed for acceptance, but harbored the wish
to put a bullet through the head of Old Man Winter.

When a savage thaw turned the streets to creeks,
I heard a great commotion on the bare maple,
a cacophony of birdsong wild and insistent,
a great collective chant. There

on sagging branches were twenty-one birds,
every one of my regulars: a pair of woodpeckers,
a pair of cardinals, and all the rest,
like Noah's Ark. I'm not one to believe in signs,

and I have no idea where my winter birds went
for one frozen week in February,
to return plump and full of fervor
to my little sanctuary and my love for them,

but that little maple will always be
my Alleluia Tree.

Listen To The Snow

The summer sedum slump, bedraggled by a bedlam of new snow,
snow so thick it bends the large lilacs and topples prairie grass.
At last the city is perfectly quiet, its recent crime wave on hold,
snow a better antidote to violence than all the men with guns.

A blizzard brings out the best in neighbors. This minute Anthony,
snow still falling gently on his blue parka, shovels the driveway
of our oldest resident, here on our quaint street where maples
hold snow on their bare limbs. Everything is closed. We settle in,

reconfiguring our day to meet the snow's agenda. Today
snow is the Boss of Everything: school, traffic, appointments,
meetings, choirs, trysts, operations, helicopters, vacations obey
snow's sweet command: Stop everything you are doing. Be still.

Adjust your entire day, so says the snow. Finish that book,
snow says. Be kind to neighbors and pets. Fill the bird feeder.
Clear your desk. Call your mother. Write this poem. Learn to wait,
snow says. Listen to the glorious complete quiet of this day.

Tomorrow, when the city has done its best to rid the pestilence of
snow, when we've had enough of snowmen and hot chocolate,
tomorrow, when things get back to normal, whatever that may be,
snow's sweet quiet will linger for a moment, then melt into

the day's business as usual. But in your bones you know
snow transforms like a powerful meditation, a great reminder
that there's something to be said for that slow silence
snow bestows on anyone who cares to listen to the snow.

Never envy the soprano.
Enjoy your own complexity:
Great harmonizer and supporter,
Middle child of the chorale,
Soothing tone-meister below the ether,
Stout-hearted Earth Mother,
Goddess of the loam,
You who make others shine.
Revel in your complicated range:
Oh you, Ms. Contrarian,
Ms. Contrapoint and Swingover,
Ms. Deep, Dark Resonance of Jazz,
Ms. Growling Blues like a Saxophone,
Ms. Mellow like Old Vine Primitivo wine.
You, whose torchy voice digs down.
Don't even think about being Julie Andrews.
Remember Rosemary Clooney,
Her voice like a mint julep on a humid day,
Or like cream in:
Peaches anda cream anda everything.
C'mon a my house, my house a c'mon.
I'm gonna giva ya everything.

Again On The Road To Tillamook

Heading west from Portland to Tillamook,
rain on the windshield,
the wipers syncopating
like the radio's jazz, your fingers
tapping the steering wheel,
and suddenly I'm whistling a riff,
rolling down the windows,
catching a cool spray
against my shoulder,
think of a question to steer us
through the mountains,
deciding on no talk: just jazz,
soybean fields rolling by,
blue mountain's rim of sun,
slash of amber cloud,
hint of moon. Then
we're really in the think of it:
Sonny Rollins,
the silence of elk.
We're blinking past Lee's Camp Store,
where the radio gives up the ghost.
All stillness and the Pacific's tug.
We have mastered this: driving
where even jazz can't follow
to the other side, a pasture of cows,
rich odor of Tillamook.
Just ahead, where we can go
no further: the sea, the sea.

The soprano, whose voice is brilliant
as fire, sings the aria from Madame Butterfly
on the radio in the Port Townsend Antique Store.

The notes build like snow before an avalanche
on Mount Baker across the bay.
This could be heaven, I am thinking,

examining the quirky Nippon vases
I háve grown fond of: the ardor of their attempts
at European Baroque foiled

by the ever-graceful elongated necks
of snow geese, the calligraphy of stylized trees.
How I love this upstart marriage of East and West.

The aria reaches its zenith when I enter
booth #23, a dark cove devoted to things *Nippon*,
the era before Pearl Harbor,

before the high society ladies scratched off
Nippon from the bottom of tea sets,
delicate and filigreed as small, old hands.

The aria reaches its zenith, which
would have been enough to fog my glasses,
enough to flood my eyes.

There on the wall a strange painting startles me.
It is so topsy-turvy, so incongruous
I am drawn into it—

a cacophony of bird wings, helter-skelter
like a firestorm, in faded read and muddy charcoal
Birds adrift like autumn leaves!

It reads: *Sparrows Falling from the Sky*,
Hiroshima, Artist Unknown.
It grips me by the throat—rain on my face.

Mango Key Lime Chutney

I tasted you and knew we could have a history:
You in cream cheese with peppercorn crackers,
or as a garnish for blackened fish. A splash of you
on an English muffin would bring back
lush days of Florida, brilliant indigo dusk
and mango sunrises.

Oh, how we would show off for company:
Your complex zest contributing
to a memorable meal, sparking
good conversation of travel and music
among kindred spirits at the table.
You were perfect in cut glass.

I didn't mind overpaying for you,
my bittersweet, succulent spread.
Wrapped in key lime colored tissue
in a lemon colored bag—why, you
could even serve as a special gift
brought home from the tropics.

So, my dear patriot, I am sorry
you have been confiscated.
Double sorry that of all I imagined of you,
weaponry wasn't in the mix.
Your bright tissue has been rolled away,
and lo, you are more than three ounces.

You, my sweet, pose an airport security threat. You!
You are being thrown into whatever witch's brew
the mango orange alert has deemed mandatory.
A Limbo of the lost and forgotten:
Cans of Ensure in every flavor,
a multitude of Lilliputian screwdrivers,

designer shampoos, a Gucci manicure kit,
fruit cocktail, St. Augustine perfume,
a monopod that looks like a billy club,
K-Y personal warming jelly, tanning oils
with varying degrees of coconut and UV protection,
a jetty of plastic bottles...

Who gets all this stuff anyway?
Do they throw a party?
How do I get invited?

At Three Arch Cape

Low tide and empty beach.
Even the mist incandesces below
Three Arches, their peaks
like primitive gods.
A faint rainbow forms
around them perfectly
like a shrine.
Last week's measured life
with its compromises
like broken sand dollars vanishes.
On the great redwood's limb
now bleached bone-gray:
our initials, JS/CS.
Who could guess a couple
married for a third of a century?
Still, today I walk alone,
head down my favorite inlet,
past the familiar shanties
and new condos rising:
misguided fortresses
that trespass shifting dunes.
No matter what – I still return,
and when I round the bend
to Netarts Bay,
the entire village, old and new,
is fodder for the fog
pierced only by pelicans.
High hum of wind and gull shriek.
Pelicans swooping.
Today this beach with its shells
and parables is my companion,
and you, drinking coffee,
reading newspapers, you're earthbound.
I'm all tides and fog.

Only give me these dreamy mornings
to keep. Let me sit again
on burnt driftwood, my back
against a dune, sing again the song
that ends in Sanctus, Sanctus.
It is enough to count myself among
the lucky, plucking perfect agates
and Holy Ghost money from sand.
And you in your blue stocking cap
and black leather jacket, waving.

Without Shoes

Henry walks into the restaurant
in stocking feet. Suddenly
his wife, son, and daughter see
that no one noticed Dad shuffling
to the old Buick, shoeless.
Dad, a child now chauffeured
in the back seat of his own car.
Now he sees that he has forgotten
his loafers.
      No one says anything.

No one knows that the daughter,
here now with the family, has been
disinherited. The family is well-schooled
in keeping up appearances, but the daughter
followed her heart and broke
the rules for Love in the Middle Class.

Later, she will be the one to pull off
his clammy white socks, rub his sallow,
calloused feet with her thumbs.
She will smooth over the balls of his feet
with the fleshy part of her palm,
kneading each foot gently. And seeing
the bulging veins, the turbulent river
of his old body, the collapsed tributaries,
and the old bones splayed like the wing
of a raven, she will rub until his feet
turn pink, as though they were embarrassed.

His feet will blush,
flushed with warmth
he hardly recognizes.
      She is
her father's daughter and will not cry.
Neither speaks an apology.
She is washing his feet
with a white washcloth
soaked in lemon-scented shampoo.
This he accepts without judgment.

Fallow

The fallow field absorbs the rain,
  which turns its soil deeper brown.
The farmer has left it unplanted
  until the elements have nourished
just the right environment for growing.
  The wise farmer does this by intention.
I remind myself of this when friendships
  strain and blow like parched topsoil.
Or when a surprising impasse enters
  a conversation or a project, I try
to leave it alone for awhile. This,
  despite what psychologists may say,
is not passive-aggression. Sometimes
  waiting is just waiting, which requires
intentional patience and hope for rain.
  I remind myself of that intentional farmer
when writer's block makes my mind shrivel
  like a dry field, sprinkled only with weeds,
not one worth picking. I have learned
  to let my mind go fallow. After all,
all things need a rest. Even marriage
  needs a recess now and then.
The trick is to lie down in your own corner
  on your own blanket and take a nap.
In marriage we are all kindergartners.
  A nap is like a fallow field,
empty and ready for renewal.
  Love that lasts will have its barren patches.
Once I planted milk pod seeds deep in the soil.
  The first year they lay fallow. Not one
sprouted in the garden. Two years later
  dozens nestled near the phlox
and sunflowers. Today monarchs lay eggs
  on milk pod leaves. Butterflies are hatching.

Necessary Adjustments

Without orthodics inserted into
almost-old-lady walking shoes,
a tendon yells at a toe.

Without monthly spinal manipulations,
shoulders and neck begin to form
a hard shell not unlike a snapping turtle's.

Without regular swimming,
the entire alignment grows weak
and dim as a retired Tinker Bell's.

Without reading glasses, the once perfect vision
sees only dust motes on bottles
and a wobbly sea of gray on pages.

Without lip wax, a caterpillar hatches,
yanked without mercy by the blonde beautician
who thinks this will never happen to her.

Without root and highlight touch ups,
salient shades of summer and autumn
give way to various shades of snow.

Let us not forget the skin, speckled
and blotched with liver spots:
an ironic record of happy days in the sun.

Somewhere on your leg is a secret map
marked with an X of tiny red and blue veins,
but no treasure hides there,

only the body with its necessary adjustments.
Yet none of this is tragic, is it?
We carry on,

thanking whatever god we know
that the goldfinch still lands on the sunflower,
that little mammals of every sort love us,

that we can still botch a house project
and have the courage to laugh at ourselves.
We thank whomever lifts and sustains us

as we obey the physics of our species,
the dialectic of the world without end,
but not without a fight.

Garden Pleasures

The hummingbird hovers
over ruby bergamot—
soft summer dusks.

Each day another swallowtail
floats by, landing on pink
cone flowers and milk pods.

At the suet, a downy woodpecker
hangs upside-down,
the chickadee rightside-up.

Cottage bound cats curl near
clumps of French lavender and
prairie grasses grown round as hay stacks.

Sparrows land on phlox.
Families of goldfinch pull out
sunflowers from feeders daily.

Butter-and-eggs bloom on wispy stalks,
and everyday for no apparent reason—
sun on lilies and black-eyed Susans.

Indigo sky at twilight—
Venus ablaze, and always
the moon in her many corsets.

Before Communion At St. Nicholas Cathedral

Perhaps it is better not knowing the words
only these voices raised a cappella
and the old woman pressing her hands
as if lifting the spirit above her
while mosaics spin like Van Gogh's Starry Night.

Perhaps it is better not knowing the words
only this rail of old faces
who have known too many words
each one a loss
what we all leave behind

until we shape an egg of them
like the oval dome surrounding us
as perfect as the wafer
wild-white and thin, ready
for the sapphire silence.

Aunt Christine's Orgasmic Salad

Begin with anticipation, curiosity,
And an herb garden. Be sure to first honor
The birds with your attention, always
Giving thanks for the day's abundanza.

Then snip the tender sprigs of chives,
Lemon-sage, plum basil, Greek oregano—
Anything whose scent sends you back to Sienna,
Samos, or your grandmother's kitchen.

Place the herbs in your trusty colander
In the sink beneath the window, where you
Can feel the sun, hear the rain, remembering
Always their contrapuntal necessities.

Spray the sprigs with ice-cold water,
Inhaling the deep green of fresh things.
Add whatever lettuce is in season—
Even ice-berg if it's crisp and pale yellow,

For no matter what they say, you need
Not be a snob regarding lettuce.
Tomatoes are another matter. Only fresh
And sweet will do. Do not be hothouse tempted.

Remember how we love the sweet crescents
Of purple onion for there is something
In their pungence that makes us feel more alive.
Eschew not the crisp, sparkling peppers

With their Frido Khalo flamboyance.
Dare to complicate with a good avocado,
A wedge of gorgonzola, a dash of fresh Romano.
Consider chopped artichokes, hearts of palm—

Those succulent gypsies dancing in a circle.
Build to a crunch climax: a splash of cashews,
Almonds, sesame seeds. For flare, slivered dates.
The secret is to be spontaneous.

Be sure to use a large, open bowl,
Salad tongs with a history,
Olive oil and balsamic vinegar (3 to 1).
Go lightly on the tender spears and leaves

For a salad's not made for puckering.
There's enough that's sour in the world
To go around. Toss—and toss with gusto
Until every leaf shines and shouts Eat me!

Go easy on the salt
For salt is like a well-meaning friend
Who sometimes spins off into dominant,
Entitled, and overbearing. Instead,

Let the potpourri of vegetables and herbs
Construct their own new identity,
Like none before—a poem that gathers steam
Rushing towards its marvelous epiphany.

Be sure to include zest, whatever
Big-hearted gesture draws you always
Toward the Zen of cooking, joy of flavorful
Munching. The ultimate relaxation.

Presidential Inauguration Ball

In Port Townsend, the tribe gathers in the field house.
Admission is a donation to the Food Bank,
a bottle of wine, and a dessert to pass.

You can wear what you want:
a Mad Hatter hat, a jester crown, orange wig,
gold spiked heels, or an ironic tuxedo.

Everyone sings "Will the Circle Be Unbroken."
We are the tribe that wove the counter-culture thread
through the red, white, and blue.

Cardboard Obamas are raised like torches.
The tribe cheers, dances, and whoops it up.
It was the 60's once. We're in our 60's now.

The circle is unbroken.

Woodstock Forty Years Later

We wandered far from flimsy, free love fantasies,
far from our deluded Dionysian debacle,
far from the Merry Pranksters and paisley busses,
so far from the Magical Mystery Tour;
slapped into the slippery muddy slopes of real life.
Oh, but what a rite of passage—
that great white walrus of Woodstock.

What I remember most was rain and mud,
walking in the muck uphill, pilgrims plopping onward
for a glimpse of freshly-minted saints and Sirens:
the major arcana of musicians, ghosts of Woodstocks past.
Pilgrims love their martyrs though we didn't know it then,
walking the counter-culture via dolorosa barefoot,
lured and charmed by our branded saints and Sirens.

But after the Siren songs and freak rains sent
us blowin' in the wind, where's home?
What happens after such a grand Chautauqua?
Where do revelers of revival and revision go?
Some wandered the desert, foraging every new manna
delivered by ever-darkening gods,
every new high, finally reaching ecstasy or death.

Some stayed in communes, like promiscuous monks,
practicing vegetarianism and free love.
Some became able to do much of nothing.
Gurus grew like grapes. Mantras spiraled like vines.
Some went to Viet Nam, Canada or jail.
Some marched until Viet Nam collapsed. Most of us moved
on into a changed world, and tried to make our way in it.

Watching the stock market go bi-polar,
I resurrected soaps pilfered from various hotels:
small fragrant bars of avocado, lemon
oatmeal, and gardenia.
The recession was upon us: time to use the soap.
Rubbing the waxy nub of talon down to nothing,
I broke out in a rash
and had to buy an expensive prescription.

Watching our retirement savings dip
into a bottomless well, I bought cheap cat food,
cheaper litter, and macaroni and cheese for $0.39.
The cats cooperated for exactly one day,
then succumbed to clinical depression.
I gave in. They ate Fancy Feast.
We ate macaroni and cheese.

I returned to substitute teaching,
cut coupons diligently, canceled trips
and acupuncture, drove less,
set the winter thermostat at 69 degrees,
and the summer thermostat at 79,
bought crappy coffee, ignored my hair,
skipped Weight Watchers, recycled my wardrobe,
and did only huge loads of laundry, cold cycle.

The coffee gave me a stomach ache.
I gained 10 pounds.
The clothes lost their zesty colors.
Gas prices climbed Mount Everest,
and an avalanche of inflation ate any savings
our meager sacrifices may have made.

There was no end to the ironies:
The Hillary engine threw a rod.
John McCain morphed into an old, angry white man,
devoured by a barracuda named Sarah Palin.
Barack Obama became President-Elect.
The stock market remained bi-polar
though bail-outs swung from trees
like howler monkeys. Yes, a crazy time
in the jungle. 2008 is over.

Last night I dreamed of an organ grinder
monkey and woke wearing a grin.
Today I scheduled acupuncture,
went to Weight Watchers,
bought delicious coffee
and lavender soap from Provence.
I have learned this: Life is too short
for bad soap and coffee. Never cancel
anything that makes you feel better.
And, if a Black man can become President
of the United States of America,
you may as well swing toward hope.

2009

Just when you thought things couldn't get worse,
the newly elected President, our Great Hope,
began an odyssey with perils lurking in every harbor,
and seas so stormy, no one could catch his breath.

Suppose you were the captain of a great sinking ship,
an economy not unlike the whirlpool of Charybdis,
with tentacles tangling your best intentions like Scylla's,
your greatest ally, Ted, sent to the Land Of The Dead.

Suppose every move you made seemed wrong,
and even your own men turned against you.
Your greatest desire, health care reform, morphed into Cyclopes,
and your only choice to wound it.

Suppose that one by one, all you counted on drifted away,
and even your prizes and honors aroused suspicion,
every attempt to restore dignity thwarted by unexpected guests,
and there you were shaking their hands.

Would you retreat to the Lotus Eaters?
Would you stuff your ears with wax when some vague Siren song
tinkled and twittered on airwaves and cell phones?
Could you steer your great ship back to home?

Numbness settled in like leftover morphine.
Inertia was a cane we limped with every day.
It was like wearing a wool coat in August,
    a heaviness we couldn't shake.
Hope was a muted light we tiptoed towards,
    always in slow motion.
Suppose they gave a Recovery Party
    and nobody came?

All over America nests fell on cement.
The eggs have cracked.
Few fledglings flew far.
Without instinct like birds'
    who leave nests naturally
    to sleep balanced on thin branches,
    we can't fly from the manifold losses
    these years have laid upon us.

Call it Deep Recession.
Call it Mild Depression.
Call it any damn thing you please.
Can we finally foreclose on grief?
Then let's foreclose on greed too,
    which we'd know, if we
    looked it straight in the face,
    brought us here in the first place.

Questions On A Long Winter Morning

Why do some people choose to live
in their wounds, milking them daily?

Pessimists are incompetent.

What defines you more:
your joys or your sorrows?

Depends on how much Oprah you've been watching.

How did cell phones take over the world
when no one was looking?

Because bees and brain cells can't fight back.

What is the difference
between a waning and a gibbous moon?

The perspective of the sun.

If a tree falls in the forest,
why is there a question about whether it fell?

Narcissists are incompetent.

If you don't believe in God,
who is the conversation in your mind with?

God.

I'm giving up.
I'm giving up Brad Pitt,
George Clooney,
in fact the entire cast
of Oceans Infinitum.
I'm giving up smelt,
horehound drops,
spam-scrambled eggs,
Belfast, and Gary, Indiana;
TV evangelists,
male enzyme enhancement,
multi-tasking, and cuckolding.
Yep, I'm giving up.
I'm giving up Tupperware,
Avon, Salad Shooter,
French nails and Astro-Turf,
Naugahyde, Colonial furniture,
and Hummels; escargot,
Kashi, and farm-fed shrimp.
Yes, I'm giving up.
I'm giving up pretending
to like Starbuck's coffee,
that I don't watch television,
and that I understand square feet.
I'm giving up Rush Limbaugh,
both Howard Sterns, and Bill O'Reilly;
ice fishing, rappelling, and hunting;
the expressions "laid back"
and "sucky" and "functionality."
I'm giving up thongs, Botox,
tanning beds, and liposuction.
You heard it here, folks.
I'm giving up.

The Chagall Windows

Perhaps it's the steeple's slanted shadows
or the way our skin still loves our bones,
how our lips don't turn down yet, even

as silhouettes in this old photo: Zurich.
Denise and I beneath The Chagall Windows.
She wears the trekking boots she kept

from the summer we spent in Mexico.
A Creole born in Martinique, now Swiss,
Denise knew several languages but rarely spoke.

She curled into herself that night
listening to Keith Jarrett's Concert at Lausanne
from speakers in her Zurich flat. Denise,

of all we ever wanted then, beauty wasn't listed.
We strayed to remote cays that promised
hammocks strung to palm trees, where any moment

we might wake to find our difficult inner journeys
rewritten in someone else's book. In Chicago,
I visit The Chagall Mural, more diminutive,

childlike beneath skyscrapers, searing wind,
horns that ricochet, Chicagoans bundled up
with fur hats, solemn and stoic as Russians.

Denise, your lover wrote to say you left,
your quietness turned to tantrums,
dishes flung in the white tiled kitchen.

He says your doctor makes you name
the anger that afflicts you like a brutal wind.
You vanish at night and your lover worries:

Zurich is not the safe and neutral place
I would remember, he adds. More raw sex
than chocolate now. But in the photo

Chagall's lamb still shimmers,
its glass fragments brighter
than a czarina's jewels. In the photo,

snapped before the piercing cold,
look how light streams from color,
look how beauty chose us unaware.

Queen Of The Night

Shrine of clouds, red halo around the moon,
opalescent obelisk enshrouded,
and Venus, just below, like a handmaiden.
Such a lyrical night on Admiralty Inlet
where I am carrying a sack full of laundry
and pocketful of quarters,
walking down a path alone here
at Fort Warden, now a park and arts center.

As if this weren't miracle enough,
as I walk up the path, returning with
clean underwear, sweet smelling and bleached,
three deer nibble grass at my cottage door.
Mother and fawn keep their distance
while the bolder young buck stands, stares,
and steps closer. I whisper and step closer too.
Brown eyes lock under the Queen of Night sky.

The buck twitches his ear, blinks
and tiptoes away. Inky clouds cover
the moon completely and all is shadow
and silhouettes. Venus gets off her knee,
traveling incognito under a cloud front
blowing into the bay. All that remains
is a foghorn, a chilly September breeze,
the vast, dreamy indigo night.

Not only the stock market swings
Like a pendulum about to crash.

A friend falls in love with sickness
Sticks close by its side,

Lets doctors try to tame it
With a shelf full of drugs.

An elder's Alzheimer's shakes her
Back and forth

Until even her body forgets
How to live.

A polar bear tries to tip-toe
On glacial ice, trickling into the sea.

A marriage wobbles
Until a wheel flies loose.

A young man graduates
From cocaine to meth to death.

A young woman who served her country
Stops the reruns in her head

By putting a bullet through it.
Swimming in a sea of volatility

Takes a strong stroke, a mighty spirit,
And grace, my friend.

May they be yours.

RE:

Renewed and refreshed, I promise to take
this energy with me through the new year.
I solemnly swear to write the poetry
I am called to write,
and when those Elysian fields
fold fallow beneath the snow,
turn my ear and eye to revision.
Replenished and reanimated, I promise
to play the piano regularly,
to relearn all that I can about resolution
and recapitulation in music and in life
from this day forth. Restored
and reinvigorated, I elect to live with
good coffee and wine, savory winter soups,
more fruit, and learn the art of ginger.
Re-opened and re-fired, I return with clarity
to my good life and my good home,
and resolve: to have the piano re-tuned,
to re-paint and re-wire the garage,
re-conquer the leaking skylight.
Re-surfacing, I promise to take care
of my health, re-appear at the heath club,
re-stock my wardrobe with brighter colors,
re-sort and refine my scarf collection.
I will redefine myself as one with a smile
that puts others at ease.
I will reserve judgments, allowing them
to reincarnate in dreams and poems.
I release all wrong done to me
into the mighty cauldron of the past,
rejoicing in each daily movement
wherever it may lead. Rekindling zest,
I will fervently try to resent or regret nothing,
reclaiming: heath, style, standing,
creativity, discipline, abundance,
contentment, and the joy of reinvention.

We are the lucky travelers
on the Good Ship Earth,
exploring those places
that as Frost once said,
"When you go there,
they have to take you in."
We are the lucky travelers
with a host of haunts to call our own,
a host of haunts to call our home,
here on our dear blue planet
where paradise is possible
now and then.
        We return
to places that set us free,
places with power to invoke
the best places in us,
where we float like magic galleons,
imaginations peaked like mountains,
where only higher vibrations intrude,
and each day is its own unguided meditation,
where complete Sabbath is
not only possible but required.

Sixty

Once my husband said,
"You can't lose something
if you already had it,"
which struck me the same way
"You want to have your cake
and eat it too" always did;
but today I think I see:
Everything you have ever had
is still there within you.
You do "take it with you."

Isn't it right that the jet fuel
of desire simmers down a bit?
Isn't it right that a cornucopia
of realized dreams is sustenance enough?
Isn't it right that today you
have already walked the dawn,
a crescent moon in the indigo sky,
frost on grass you gingerly tread
in your sturdy white walking shoes?
And next, the sun, as always.

Perhaps it's Pluto's transit
or a mild case of entropy
or maybe your eyes don't refuse to see
the old men bagging groceries
in January—
     red knuckles grasping
at control, usefulness,
this paper bag labeled Work Ethic
about to rip down the middle
while green-haired grandsons
wear ragged, clown Bermudas in the snow,
eat only food that requires no utensils,
   and whine
   all the way to the mall.

Perhaps it's Mercury in Retrograde
or a terminal case of mid-life crisis
or just some hot, chocolate-covered
   Karma
when the perfect summa cum laude Princess
who's been married to Prince Charming for twenty years
dumps him for a frog
who's much more interesting on his motorcycle.
She's wearing a black leather Harley vest,
popping Rolling Rock into her cart.

It could be Neptune in the first house
or a major case of had-it-up-to-here
or just some hot, creamy goddess worship
when at least two
glory-to-god-and-motherhood
crones suddenly shear their hair
shop together, declare
the papaya looks delicious this time of year.

Under Neptune

In the arthroscopic photos
my husband's knee looks like Neptune.
The cartilage creates debris
like a comet lodged
deep within the walls of the patella,
creating unwanted microscopic mountains
and valleys where no streams can go.
The cartilage receives little or no
blood flow and cannot repair itself.

The arthroscopic astronaut,
   the surgeon,
excises the disturbing debris,
the fractious fragments,
and with luck,
my husband's life will be better for it.

Neptune is the planet of ether mysticism
or delusion.
The anesthesiologist, the god of ether,
puts a mask over my husband's mouth,
sending him into orbit in the netherzone.
If all goes well,
he will return to earth quickly,
without space sickness or other side effects.

My husband makes a safe landing
and sips ginger ale under a blue blanket
in the recovery room. For a moment,
I believed the nurse is an angel,
for I float in an atmosphere
of celestial relief. The surgeon,
who could now be Zeus himself, arrives
with the photos that began this poem,

and I thought of Neptune, remembering
the astrologer who declared
"You have Neptune in the first house!
   You live in La-La Land."

I'm here to say the La-La Land's
not so bad when you consider
the alternatives.

The very same night,
I sang the Siren song from "Neptune"
with a chorus hidden
in the ethereal wings of the grand theater
just before a standing ovation.

Delusional or not, I just love
all the quirky, quantum coincidences
colliding like space splinters
here, there, and everywhere. Amen.

Going Quebecois in Saint Agathe

In Saint Agathe, the Quebecois blue sky snuggles
the round mountains that dip into the lake.
The bells of Saint Agathe Cathedral echo.

In Saint Agathe, I buy lavender linen spray from Provence
at a boutique painted sky blue, meditate in the church
whose walls and ceiling match the Quebecois blue sky,

salute the Madonna in her starry gold crown,
and Saint Agathe, the patron saint of bell founders,
wet nurses, weavers, the hungry, and breast disease.

I thank the Madonna that there are still places
where the money changers haven't taken over,
where violence is so gauche that it isn't even imagined,

and the biggest crime committed is a faux pas—
usually by a traveler like me who can't speak French,
but ooh-la-la, finds Quebec très bien, très bien.

Instead Of Destiny

Destiny is the seed deep within the secret
revealed when colors and textures can be discerned
through the speckled lens of time's wide aperture.

Of seeds, shapes, and textures:
how about those heirloom tomatoes?
Cheyenne blacks, golden pineapple,
fuzzy peach, green-striped—
the bulbous and beautiful aborigines
of the farmer's market.

Destiny arrives in slices—
succulent, juicy glimpses
of patterned purpose,
metered messages from whatever
Mercury you tango with.

This is just to say
I have sliced the heirloom tomatoes
that you bought at the farmer's market today.
No need to forgive me.
There's plenty left for you.
So sweet with just a little salt.

Destiny is like a secret heirloom
that hides in plain sight
in the dark attic you climb to one winter day.
You say, O my. What's this?
I have the prefect place for you.

O my. I set out to write a poem
all about destiny. The urgent
heirloom tomatoes slivered in instead.

Paradigm Shift In The Pacific Northwest

In the Victorian Era rich people taxied boats
to great arched rocks just to shoot puffins
from their nests. Even the women aimed rifles
at the flaming orange, gross beaks,
hard to miss, dropping the birds
into slashing waves that swooshed and whirled
the dashed bodies out to sea. For pleasure. Sport.

Today we tilt toward Orcas whales,
hoping for a breach or spy-hop, eager
for the brilliant black and white crests,
the bold dorsal fins in sync, circling, circling
like the great gears of a grandfather clock.
We lean nearly overboard, armed with binoculars
for but a blink of calf with mother.

We stand in honor of killer whales, our secret
collective wish that one will break the law of distance
imposed off the coast of Discovery Island, here
in the San Juan de Fuca Straits, where we funny folks
in hats and hoods hope a curious killer whale forgives us.
Come closer. Come closer. Our collective prayer:
Don't leave us now. We'll make amends. Come closer.

The Red Lacquer Room
for Lynda Hull

We were hiding in the Red Lacquer Room,
the empty dance floor of the grand old Palmer House
deep in the center of Chicago with its black canyons,
dark sky scrapers, faint friction, sparks of the El
clambering like a craving. You said I'd be surprised
how you had lost your beauty. Thin

as a refuge, your black and blue babushka twirled
into a turban, high Bohemian style, you seemed
more like a ragged survivor than the gypsy that you were.
Dear Lynda, even when we dared
flick on the great white chandeliers
of the Red Lacquer Room, I knew the streets

had won but pretended we crouched together
in a lovely surreal dream where happy endings
bright as crystal chandeliers in ballrooms still glow.
I thought surely you might find a way past
the city's chaos, the jagged graffiti, the stone souls.
I thought you might find stillness in the lake's

lapping tongues, a lilting gull, some small place
not quite ecstasy. No, you could never
be consoled by compromise, or live slowly
to keep an ending less violent: that slippery slope
in winter near Provincetown. The fatal crash.
Gone too, the Red Lacquer Room's sparkling lights.

Lynda, know that when I think of you
I still see envelopes of poems crossing the Atlantic
jet streams from the Heartland to Barcelona
where a dark Siren song lured you to a strange park
full of circus mirrors at the edge of town.
Sometimes distortion is all the magic we have.

No matter. To me you will always be
my muse, my mentor, my mirror,
my dark mistress of the gypsy jazz night.

This Thanksgiving, Remember

Remember the air that made the clouds that made the rain
that watered the ground and made the potatoes
both white and sweet at your Thanksgiving table.

Remember the birds that gave the eggs that gave the meat
that baked in the oven and smelled divine
surrounded by sage dressing at your Thanksgiving table.

Remember the sun that fed the vines that made the wine
the went into long-stemmed glasses and shimmered
near the candles at your Thanksgiving table.

Remember the migrants who picked the lemons that you
slice in the water with ice, and who carried the pumpkins that
whipped into the pie at your Thanksgiving table.

Remember the cows for all their kindnesses: the cream,
the milk, the cheese, and the chocolate that finished
the meal at your Thanksgiving table. Dare not forget:

All pilgrims who seek the higher life in strange
and wonderful places. All the invisible faces
of those gone on, the homeless, and the struggling,

our blue planet, that most special place in the universe,
where we the lucky thrive amidst rivers and orchards,
where fruit hangs in perfect abundant globes.

At Lake Crescent, Washington

Suppose you find yourself in some in-between space,
where no doors are clearly marked:
Enter here, you who would move forward.
Suppose even the currents of your body lost their way,
and strange manifestations disturbed the waters of your blood,
disrupted the electric currents of your heart,
beating faster than a tom-tom in a wild warrior dance.
The chaos of your pulse and loadstones of fatigue
confuse you in contrapuntal castigations.
Then you might seek a lonely, ravaged place
where two mountains meet at Lake Crescent,
a narrow passageway between them.
Let yourself be ferried on shimmering glacial water
through a narrow portal no matter where it leads.
Know that when you pass through *in-between*
you finally find *serene.*

Port Townsend Food Co-Op

A sense of intention permeates the aisles,
a supposition turned into a reality,
a trend transformed into a staple.

Here staples do not clamor for attention,
but in their lovely, still bins beckon
an invitation to health.

Here simplicity is elegant,
and a quiet post-consumer joy
whispers, "It's time. It's time."

It's time to care where food comes from,
who processed it, how, and why;
time to measure what we take from the earth.

Here food is science, art, and spirit:
Port Townsend Bay Organic Coffee,
smooth blend to start your day with a purr,

red dried apricots to keep the engine running smooth;
crunchy trail mix to sustain the engine.
So many raw, virginal foods to keep it revved!

This is a place that returns to a gusty palette
of dark, delicious, strong cheese,
a cornucopia of untainted vegetables,

a grinder for fresh cashew or almond butter,
a juice bar where a burst of sun and ginger
keeps the pipes rolling like STP.

A meal here has a different kind of class:
honey-roasted golden beets with a little crunch,
purple, orange and green garbanzo salads.

People arrive on bikes and with dogs
in patriotic bandanas who wait
as they shop carefully for clove shampoo,

toothpaste free of toxins and full of herbs,
talking to friends in aisles, in
a post-consumer community, where everyone

knows that having too much
no longer defines success, and happiness
shines in the sheer harmony of living well.

Should you find yourself un-sprung
by grief, like cranking gears
of the old grandfather clock
you must rewind forward each half hour
no matter what the time,
know: You can't cheat grief.
If so, you'd skip a chime,
which might end up as an extra heartbeat.
Yours. Plus—you'd have to start again.

Once I tried to cheat grief
claiming to detach from it,
jetting off to the Big Sky,
leaving grief at home on my pillow.
When I looked up at the Seraut sky,
I felt the dead I cherished,
wept mercilessly under the Milky Way,
each shooting star
someone I would never see again.

Stone With Hole

you will find me
holding up the pillars
of Chichen Itza or Alexandria
I am the parrot's eye of Easter Island
seventeen Indians polished me
ground out this hole
which you peer through now
the curve of my side
is like the curve in yours
your dry hip bone
bleached gleaming
in another world

The Big Easy

When the plane descends over Lake Pontchartrain,
I look into the waters from the window seat.
A miasma rises with the haze on murky water.
A small white boat floats like a femur alone
near the thin, white bridge which vanishes into the fog.

I am stunned by the ghosts who greet me
here in the Big Easy, where nothing is easy anymore.
All through the trip I try to name them:
the old waiter from Antoine's,
the missing drummer in the street trio,
the tap dancing brother displaced in San Antonio.

At the convention, the food is strangely cold,
laissez faire. Coffee is never served.
The staff is small, untrained, unsmiling.
Katrina and betrayal hang in the air
like the relentless and fierce summer humidity
as hurricane season begins.

From my window I see a storm brewing
like voodoo over the Mississippi,
hear thunder sputter like demons,
keenly aware that just around the river's bend,
the lake with its unsure levies sits
like the cruelest of Roman emperors.

Where are they?
Belle, the lavatory matron, setting out gardenia cologne.
Willard, the antique store clerk, with his dog, Bella.
Teneesha, whose house has never been rebuilt.
Zydeco Man afloat in another city.

Friday night in the French Quarter pulses with hope.
A band of black teenagers blows tight jazz
on the corner of Canal and Chartres.
The beat drives us forward. We begin to dance.

At dinner an impromptu Dixie band
plays *When the Saints go Marching in.*
I feel them, the unnamed saints, marching,
as the good times begin to roll again,
marching, slow and soulful,
the trumpet wailing like a banshee.
The wind screams like spirits doomed to wander
until they find a resting place.

the killer poet would drive a black '37 Ford
like a fiend down Michigan Avenue, rutting
up alleys, past blue cats that shimmer
in window sills, backing right into
his puffy-faced stepfather. Then
the car would vanish,
and they would run
on the ledge of the Sears Tower
until the killer poet faces the stepfather
and pushes him over for keeps.
If dreams wrote the story
green pills would ooze
from the killer poet's mouth
until he spits them out
and leaps for joy, balancing
like a tight-
rope walker as the ledge
morphs into an ice-escalator.
Then the killer poet would know:
all he has to do to ride it
down is to stand
still.

The Shrink Or The Poet?

To the Shrink symbols are sacraments:
ritualistic, dogmatic, powerful.
Tight Shoulders = Shouldering Responsibilities.
A man who visits his mother
instead of going to a party = Repressed.
Overeating = Sublimation, Stuffing,
Suffering, Lack of Voice.

The poet juggles symbols like a fire-thrower
in the indigo Quebecois night,
where every little thing is subject to interpretation:
A glass of garnet red claret might be life blood,
Holy Communion, love rekindled or love unleashed.
Tight shoulders might mean grasping the headboard
during love in a place where sublimation
is only a word as dry as bread without butter.

The Shrink has a convenient word for every state of the soul,
and for every state of the soul pathology exists:
Take Depression (the trailer park cousin of Melancholy,
who lives in castles rich with burgundy Damask curtains),
always someone to avoid.

The poet will have her dark night of the soul,
emerge as a phoenix, a winged tiger.

As the Shrink understands, clarifies, and (yes) shrinks
the soul into bite-size pieces of a puzzle,
the poet experiences, risks and suffers consequences,
embracing the puzzle that can't be squarely solved.
The Shrink thinks he is putting the square peg
in the square hole

but the poet knows better.

Changing Names

Today in San Francisco I meet a young man
with flaming red hair
who says his name is Sweet Pea.
He's reinvented himself from Bobby,
the boy bred in Wisconsin.
Then I meet Yarrow, also reinvented,
once Michelle of Pennsylvania.
A tunnel opens in my brain
where the reinvented people are stored:
Shannon, who became Subatra;
or the middle-aged woman I remember who changed
her name from Jane (which reminds me of Jane Eyre)
to Lovelight (which reminds me of the Summer of Love);
or the string of newly named Anandas like prayer beads;
quirky hyphenated surnames:
Black-Cowing, Liddle-Cox, Page-Tierning.
I wish them all god-speed in their quest for reinvention,
yet wonder what happens when you trade
a saint's name for a flower, a Celtic name
with a long tradition
for an exotic name with an esoteric meaning.
Can you exorcise family demons
or do they follow anyway?
If I changed my name to Lavender,
would my poems be sweet and dreamy?
Would that make them better?
If you changed your name to Dancing Wind,
could you be a shaman, a better dancer?
Could you whoop through someone's Dream Catcher?

The Ladies in Black

huddle on the main street of town
   each day.
The Zen rain chants on their
   black umbrellas.
The coven continues
   every day
and will not stop until perfect
   peace prevails
and all native sons and daughters
   safely return.
When I see the Ladies in Black
   with only
the soft staccato of the rain on their
   black umbrellas,
I am completely stirred
   and sorrowed,
the way a surprising poem
   might grip me,
or the way I roil when I see photos
   of mothers
who have lost children
   in cross-fire.
Within us all is a Lady in Black,
   designated mourner,
keeper of rage, reminder of compassion.
   Within you
is a potent negative capability,
   a deep
bleak place, palpable and capable.
   May you
never lose your will, great ladies.
   May monsoons
of victory break your umbrellas.
   May you
dress in brightest colors—and swing.

Study In The Overuse Of Alliteration

When your bucket of blunders burdens you,
bury it n the garbage bin,
tie it with a tight bow and let it go.

If your mantel of mistakes manages to outmaneuver you,
clear it off, box the contents
and send it out to the Salvation Army.

So your snarling sack of snafus starts to out do you?
Un-snake and unravel each strand.
Then shred them all for good.

Dare the darlings of delusion dwell too long,
deliver them from their disappointment.
Close the lid and dump them.

Should certain cares come to crush you,
crash them like a tsunami
or simply create compost of them.

Whenever worms of worry wiggle into your
peace of mind, wind a hook through them
and feed them to the walleyes.

When on occasion the black obelisk of obstacles
hangs over your head like a piñata,
punch it with a pole until it spills its gifts.

The pendulum of problems probes too close?
Prime yourself in the knowledge
that is will surely swing back.

Know that even a random universe
has checks and balances, its cosmic dialectic.
Know: Chaos doesn't last forever.

Dear Masseuse

You have turned
my toes to velvet mushrooms,
my arches to cotton,
the balls of my feet to Indian drums,
my heels to onyx,
my ankles to pigeon feet,
my calves to oranges,
the back of my knees to creeks,
my thighs to bread dough,
my lumbar to stars,
my spine to piano keys,
my shoulder blades to foothills,
my shoulders to satin ribbon,
the crimp of my neck to root,
my neck to stem,
my head to dandelion,
my hair to fluff,
scattered in the eucalyptus wind.

The Pleasures Of Wine

I love the poetry of wine tasting:
  Bouquet, nose, dark earth tones, smooth finish.
The colors please and dazzle:
  Ruby red, soft gold, plum-indigo, dusty pink.
The names of the wine delight the ear:
  Claret, Gamay, Merlot, Chardonnay, Chianti.
They take you back to places you love,
  Escort you to places you want to go:
The South of France, Tuscany, Napa and Sonoma.

I love learning the complications and nuances:
  Old Vine Zinfandel, darker and duskier
Than its trailer park cousin, pink Zinfandel.
  Pinot Noir more delicate than dime-store Rosé.
How a Cuvee can startle the palette with complexity,
  And a Primitivo takes you back to the earth itself.
Thousands of vineyards spawn stranger names than
  Literary magazines: Smoking Loon, Red Truck, Bellagio.
Bolla, Villages, Blue Moon, Yellow Tail, St. Michelle.

I love the sophistication of complementary pairing.
  It's a harmonic symphony and contrapoint of flavors:
Tuna Nicoise with a refreshing, dry Pinot Grigio.
  Apples and cheddar with St. Francis Old Vine Zinfandel.
Crusty bread and Swiss with a bold Chianti Classico.
  Chilled Muscat with strawberries and cream on the patio.
Port or Sherry by the fire on a cold, winter day.
  Dark, bitter chocolate with Framboise in a tulip glass.
Sweet blackberry wine drizzled on fruit compote.

I love the hints of the sacred surrounding wine:
  The long-stemmed glass, like a chalice.
The lifting and swirling to celebrate color.
  The deep breath and suspense of the first bouquet
To identify the subtle smells of oak, tannin, cherry, earth.
  The first sip swirled down the tongue and throat.
The savoring, pronouncements and comparisons.
  The camaraderie amongst the wine aficionados.
The round, white wafers to cleanse the palette between wines.

I love shopping for wine bargains in unlikely warehouses
  Where the uninitiated walk past unknowingly,
 Where a 2004 Rutherford Hill Cabernet Sauvignon
  Might be in the sale bin for a scandalously low price,
Or an entire case of Mum Cuvee Champagne has been ignored.
  Or there is a sudden close-out on Cotes du Rhone.
What pleasure in adding these to the basement wine rack.
  What pleasure in opening one for dinner, pumping the corkscrew,
The lively pop, your smile when you come home from work.

At The Sacred Cliffs of Kauai

No matter how wide nor deep
today's grief, remember:
the world is wider and deeper.
When you feel it shrinking, know:
new earth still forms,
volcanic fire on the sea.
There may come a time when
things won't get better,
but not today
with its cleansing rain,
its hope of rainbows,
its change of plans.
Even the planets retrograde
and don't fall from their orbits.
In a million years, the Na Pali cliffs
will be nothing but a coral reef,
but see how they do nothing
to speed their erosion. Be like that.
Stand hard in your grief,
and let elements pound your ribs,
carve out something solid,
a jagged beauty unsurpassed,
pierced and pointing to the sacred.

How To Be Happy In Old Age

Refer to Pavarotti as your friend.
Listen to him often.
Try to live the way he sings.
Give everyone A's in everything.
Never be afraid of your hair
or what others might say about it.
Prefer levity to pomposity.
Make up wonderful lies
especially to stupid questions.
Love good food and drink.
Cook marvelously.
Carry a rusty briefcase
or a red knapsack.
Make satirical weathervanes.
Wear outrageous socks.

Manifesto To The Health Police

Sorry, I don't want to dine
with the gluten police,
the peanut patrol,
the red meat comrades
or the sugar Nazis.
Do not say the words
sulfates, palm oil, trans fat,
or cholesterol
when we are about to engage
in the lovely restaurant ritual
of being served something special.
Sure, I'm all for organic food,
and you might be surprised
at what a healthy cook I am,
and if we were trading recipes
and not in this restaurant
I have been looking forward to all week,
where people are trying to forget
their daily strife and constrictions,
I might be interested.
But sipping red wine from Argentina,
where who knows what laws the vintners answer to,
about to help myself to the coconut shrimp
I've been saving up for all week,
I'd prefer you talk about something else.
Fascinating as you think it is,
I don't want to know your LDL's,
your resting metabolism,
or anything that begins with My Doctor.
Know that if you talk about your plastic surgery,
remotely suggesting that I should join
the ranks of the reconstructed or recently tweaked,
you will lose me as a friend.
Oh, and if you plan to badger the overworked waitress,
expecting her to know all the ingredients
that went into tonight's special,
please don't invite me.

I woke this morning from a dream of chanting
   and for a few blessed seconds, bliss enshrouded me
like the protective cocoon of a giant swallowtail.

In the dream I saw the chant—straight dark lines
   like a series of dashes. I heard the chant sung,
a clear, steady bell of voices in unison.

I entered the chant, walking through a white door.
   I wanted to stay in that sacred state,
where my entire life had finally led. Yet

I was not disappointed when I awoke enclosed
   in a blue blanket, a pillow folded beneath
my head, and the day still before me.

Cottage By The Sea

Some say the streets of heaven are lined with gold.
Give me a cottage by the sea.

Some love the lurid jingle-jangle of casinos.
Just give me a cottage by the sea.

They can have their gated communities and condo police.
I'll take a cottage by the sea

with bright colored walls and painted wicker,
treasure troves of recycled furniture,

vintage fabric and funky lampshades.
They can have their granite counters,

cookie cutter renovations a la hardware chic.
I prefer a cottage by the sea.

They can have their square footage and sprinklers.
Let me rest in my cottage by the sea.

why I write poetry,
and though I've dreamed of this moment
for years, it still stops me like a siren.
Because Mayan women do not weave chevrons
in desert sunset threads
because it is no longer useful.
Because the snowy egret leaves its marsh forever.
Because people closest to me suffer.
Because words are bread.
Because writing it is map-less as driving back roads.
Because without it, my life is measured in paychecks.
Because I love you and can't tell you.
Because I couldn't stop even if I wanted to.
Because there are so many questions nobody asks.
Because someone wants to know.

Vincent

At first it is obsession: Van Gogh painting as no one else did,
painting until he is the seed in Sunflowers,

the star in Starry Night, swabbing the deck of his palette
with child fingers, licking cobalt blue,

primary yellow, bringing them to his lips until color
sticks to the roof of his mouth

like a communion wafer, dabbing and drying
like Christ's lips touched vinegar.

Art is not religion, he is warned. But to be an artist means
to break all the rules. Do we demand such chronologies

of madness, finally exhausting ourselves discovering how
little the hidden reveals about the unknown,

no matter how compelling the color or technique?
At last he thinks he is God. He says,

We are all God, self-portrait after self-portrait,
paint like crusty worms,

resurrection at Sotheby's, then ascension
into the Big Money.

Crescent moon through fog.
Foghorn and eye of lighthouse.
Port Townsend Bay Organic Coffee in my cup.
Where will this day lead?

Here I am at last
In the colorful cottage of my dreams
On an ocean bluff
Above a blue bay

Across from Mount Baker's white, wizard hat
In a place where only poetry and music
Are required of me.
Where will this day lead?

Writing In The Dark

You have been writing in the dark
before dawn, when suddenly you discover

you are in the middle of a metaphor:
Writing in the dark before dawn,

you are waiting for illumination
or maybe just a clue

telling you that this dark muse
who has eclipsed your waning

and your fullness
was worth your attention.

By the time you read this, the dawn
has exchanged stars with the night.

Everything You Ever Wanted

One day you may wake up to find
you have everything you need.

What, then, is
 this stirring inside you?

Perhaps, like the Dalai Lama,
your soul is gathering forces
for its next incarnation,
or maybe the urge to refine
right here,
right now,
manifests on this good planet.

Could be you are part
of a windy current
flying above the jet streams to
nirvana,
or another current
has simply sent you skating
past a sociological dream
into a post-consumer world.

I read once that the Danish
are the happiest people in the world.
They live in a dark climate
eclipsed by winter.
They ride bicycles
and eat lots of ice-cream,
have less sex and suicide
than the Swedes.

They have less divorce, violence,
use of guns, anti-depressants,
locks,
and religion than we do.
They have higher taxes,
and socialized medicine.
They are not gobbling up the earth
or each other.

One day they woke up

to find
 they have everything
that they ever wanted.

Acknowledgements

Grateful acknowledgement is given to the publishers of the following journals, anthologies, presses, newspapers, and contests in which these poems first appeared, sometime in different form:

AMERICAN MASSAGE JOURNAL: *Dear Masseuse*

CHIRON REVIEW: *Fallow*; *The Shrink or the Poet?*; *Writing in the Dark*; *The Contessa and I*

CLARK STREET REVIEW: *The Big Easy*; *Going Quebecois*; *Manifesto to the Health Police*

FARMER'S MARKET: *If Dreams Wrote the Story*

FOX CRY REVIEW: *Woodstock*; *Listen to the Snow*

HAMMERS: *Rearview Mirror*

JANE'S STORIES IV: *Bridges*

KNOWING STONES: ANTHOLOGY OF EXOTIC TRAVEL: *Stone with Hole*

KORONE: *A Friend Asks*

LILOPOH: *Paradigm Shift in the Pacific Northwest*; *At the Sacred Cliffs of Kauai*; *The Alleluia Tree*

LOUISVILLE REVIEW: *The Secret of a Happy Alto*

MERIDIAN ANTHOLOGY OF CONTEMPORARY POETRY: *Mango Key Lime Chutney*; *The Pleasures of Wine*; *At the Sacred Cliffs of Kauai*; *The Ladies in Black*; *Entering the Chant*

MID-AMERICA REVIEW: *Garden Pleasures*

MINOTAUR: *Port Townsend Inauguration Ball*; *Lament for the Silent Sister*; *2008*; *Volatility*; *Instead of Destiny*; *2009*; *Again, on the Road to Tillamook*

MISSISSIPPI VALLEY REVIEW: *The Chagall Windows*

OUT OF LINE: *This Thanksgiving, Remember*; *Without Shoes*; *Sparrows Falling from the Sky*

PENINSULA REVIEW: *Moonbeam and Starlock*

PENINSULA PULSE: *The Red Lacquer Room*

PLAINSONGS: *You're the One*; *Sixty*

POETSWEST: *Piano Lessons*; *2009*; *Again, on the Road to Tillamook*; *At Three Arch Cape*

PORT TOWNSEND FOOD CO-OP NEWSLETTER: *Port Townsend Food Co-Op*

RED SILK: *Necessary Adjustments*; *Study in the Overuse of Alliteration*

ROCK RIVER TIMES: *Aunt Christine's Orgasmic Salad*; *Lament for the Silent Sister*; *RE*; *This Year for Lent*; *Questions and Questions on a Long Winter Morning*; *Perseverance*
SPOON RIVER QUARTERLY: *Nightshift*
SEVERSON DELLS NEWSLETTER: *Listen to the Snow*
STRONG COFFEE: *Ten Minutes of Michigan Avenue*
SOUNDINGS: *Woodstock Forty Years Later*; *Everything You Ever Wanted*; *Port Townsend Food Co-Op*
TRADESWOMAN: *Nightshift*
WILLOW REVIEW: *Vincent*
WISCONSIN POETS' CALENDAR 2012: *Listen to the Snow*

With special thanks to Centrum Center for the Arts, Port Townsend, WA, for residencies in which many of these poems were first written; to Frank Schier of *Rock River Times* and J. Glenn Evans of *PoetsWest* for their continuous support all these years.

A select few of these poems were first published in former collections including:

TONIGHT ON THIS LATE ROAD (Erie St Press)
INVISIBLE STRING (Erie St Press)
SLOW MIRACLE (Lake Shore Publishing)
BREAD UPON THE WATERS (Windfall Prophets)
THE TENDERNESS OF MEMORY (Plainview Press)
THE RED LACQUER ROOM (Chiron Press)
WHO WALKS AMONG THE TREES WITH CHARITY (Wind Publications)
EMBRACE UNCERTAINTY AS A CLOUD (Neville Museum)

About the Author

Christine Swanberg is all a modern poet should be.

She is the author of nine books and has had over 300 poems published in various books and journals. Her work has appeared in over sixty literary journals. She appears in a wide range of poetry anthologies.

She currently writes a column for the *Rock River Times*, a newspaper in her home town of Rockford, Illinois, that reaches 20,000 people each week.

She has a long list of poetry awards and has been an editor for various presses and magazines. She has lead a full literary life.

This is a collection of poems that contains her full circle of work. Many of the newer poems return to the simple language and construction of her earliest work. The poems in this volume span more than a third of a century.

She has had several residencies in Port Townsend, WA. She is a regular workshop leader at The Clearing, in Door County, Wisconsin.

But there is also a person behind the poetry.

Christine holds degrees from the University of Wisconsin, Rockford College and Northern Illinois University. She had a thirty year teaching career. She has a gallery in her home, *The Prints and the Poet*, where she has workshops, readings, and displays the work of her photographer husband, Jeffrey Swanberg, who was gracious enough to contribute one of his fine photographs for the cover of this book.

Her life is filled with pet rescue, gardening, swimming, and singing with several community choruses. She and her husband are world travelers with a flair for the exotic and have spent a lot of time away from the Midwest, where they live a deceptively simple life surrounded by an English garden, trees, and Chris's beloved birds.

THE PUDDIN'HEAD PRESS

Publisher and distributor of fine books

CURRENT TITLES

For more information and a complete catalog contact us:

Puddin'head Press
P. O. Box 477889
Chicago IL 60647
(708) 656-4900
(888) BOOKS-98 (orders only)

www.pudddinheadpress.com
phbooks@att.net